Soul Nourishment

Expressionism Photography

Copyright © 2018 by Dana Gregory

All rights reserved. No part of this book may be reproduced, scanned, or distributed in any printed or electronic form without permission

First Edition July 2018

Printed in the United States of America

ISBN-13: 978-1722779580
ISBN-10: 1722779586

Preface

"Women are the nourishing power of the universe, whoever has respect for women, will remain free from diseases"-Amit Ray

The journey inward of respecting the classics of rhyme and reason of mother nature is the women who are responsible for maintaining this feature here on earth. It begins as a child and it too can unravel the purest of hearts when reason has no meaning inside of values. We as women know that we must climb in and nourish the world and that is our responsibility and the male energy is there to respect the nurturing energy and grow with the women here on earth but also, to give the protection needed for the women's growth. Then the male is fed the nourishment from his guidance of protecting the beautiful power of mother nature within the universe. The universe grants gifts for the values given back to the earth's atmosphere.

The power of the human consciousness energy is consumed with multiple focused energies everywhere and yet, we are struggling to keep things in order, but the balance of mother earth is changing into the elements of change. This change is going to make us and bring unity back within the surface or it will completely divide us, and we no longer exist on mother earth. It's always up to us to make changes, as a single or as a unit.

The challenge is making changes within our own makeup of the character within. The side stepping is good for helping the angle of comfort level and it also gears us in also making another approach to life from just walking a different step, along side the critical people among us.

I simply just try to express a form of transitioning the mind from one value to another through my expressionism photography. My point of view is unique regarding the psychology of words through the artwork. Changing the eye to see the world from a different point of view then one can open the mind to change.

My hope is that it helps you in something that you are working on within yourself and give you another side step to grow, because we are all seeds growing inside of the world. Change your seed and you grow another world from just your own unique style/character. Let's see what deep inside of you and watch the flower bloom inside.

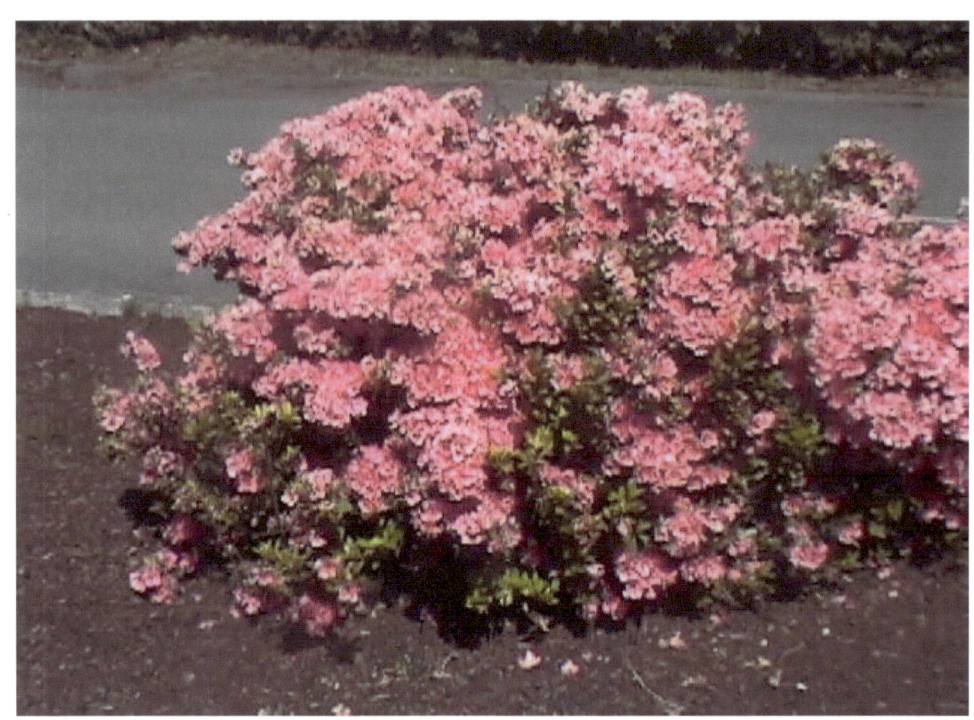

Signals of Communication

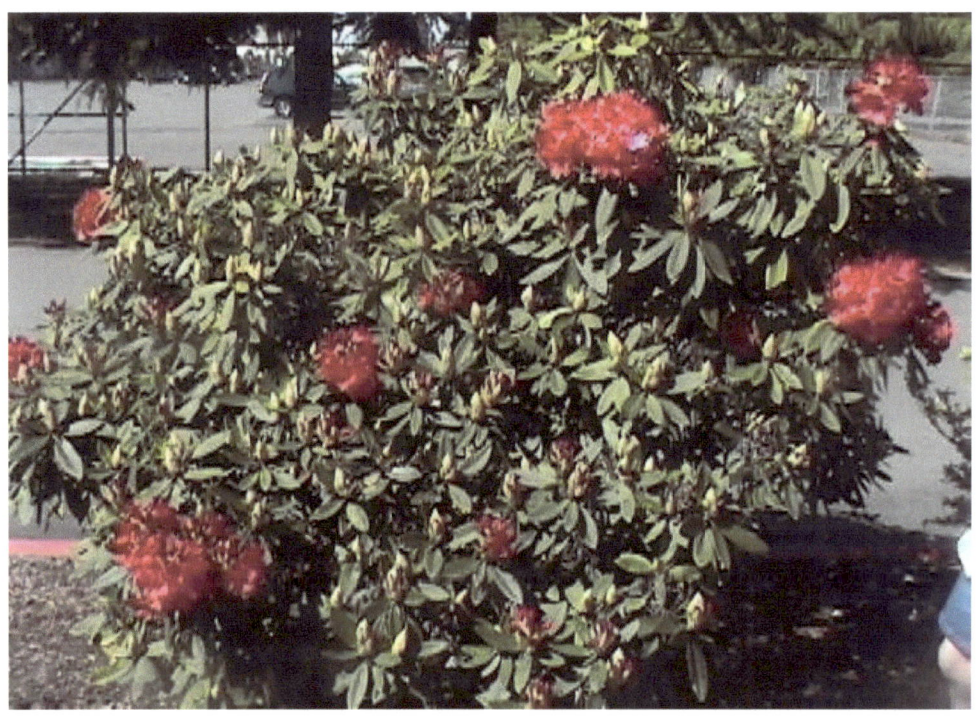

Grounding Within

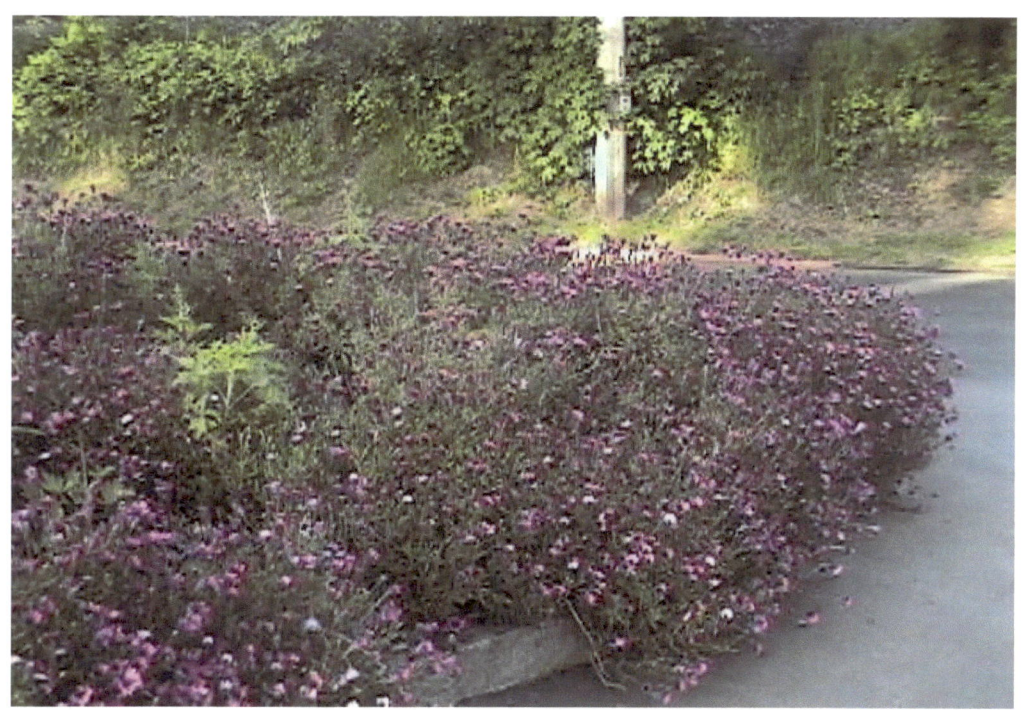

Cosmic Purple Dance

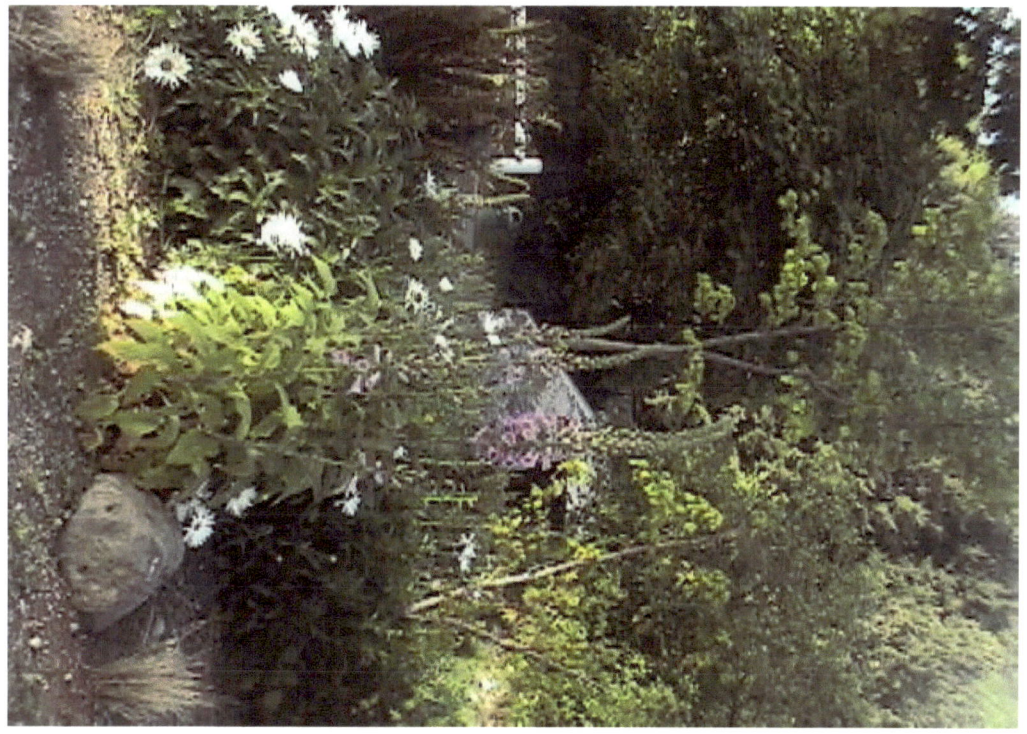

Light Bounce Inward to Right

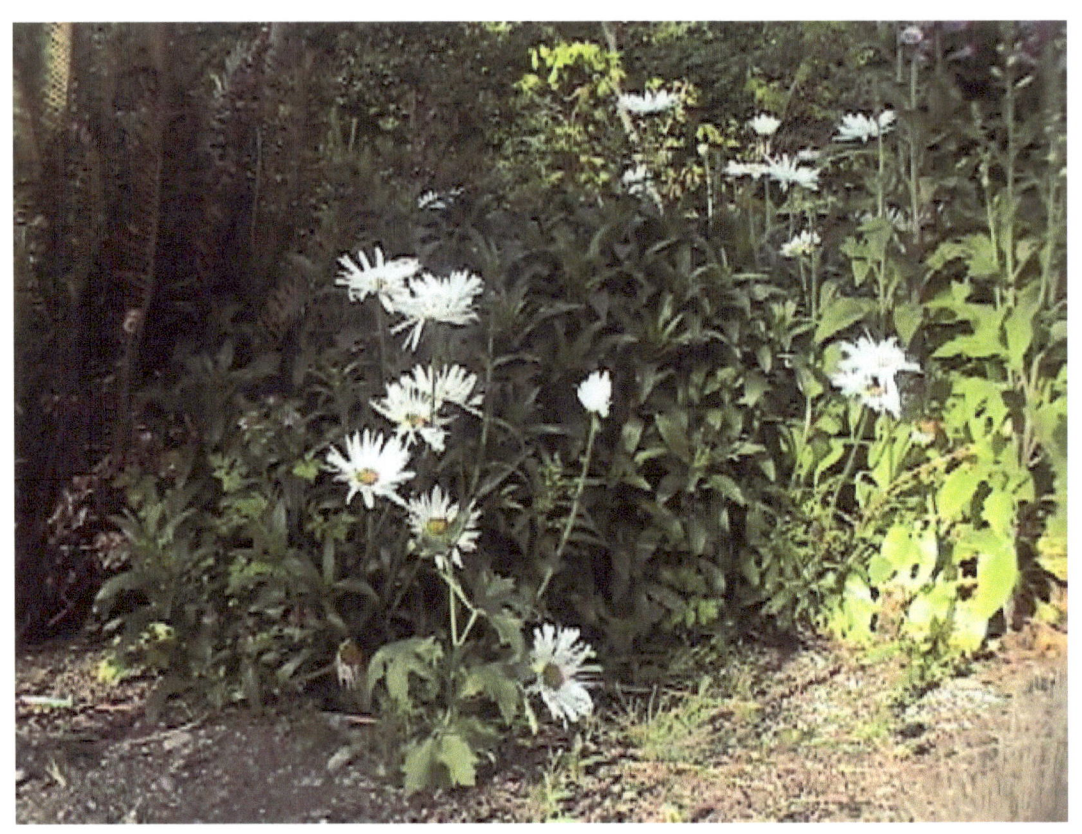

Reinforced Delicate Stance

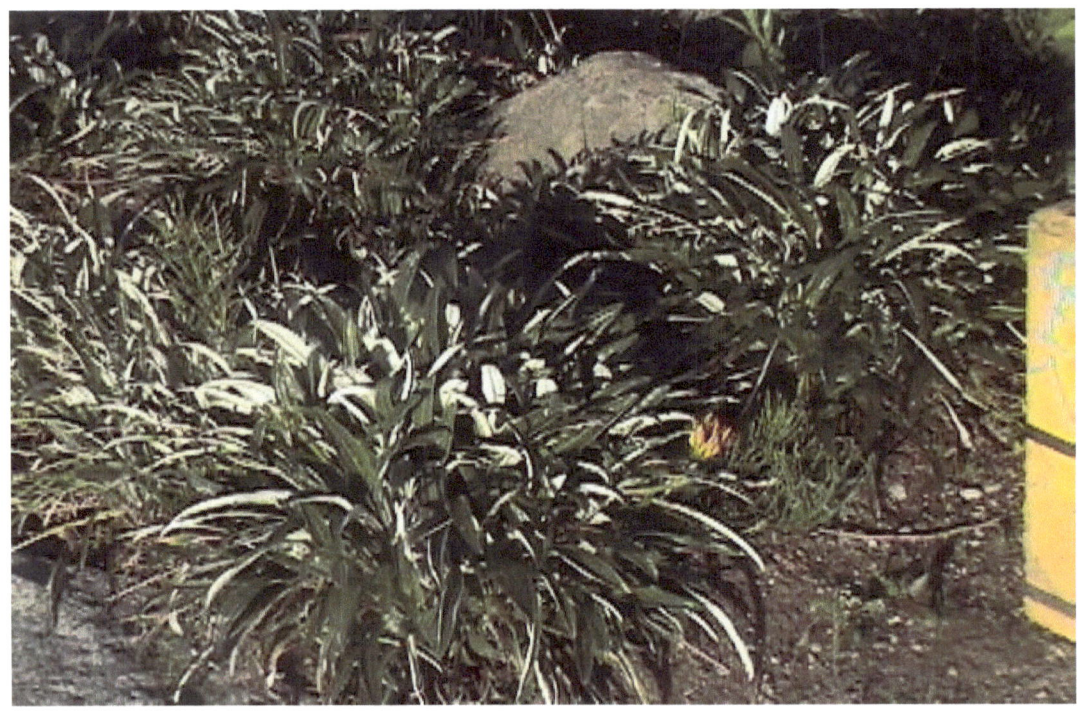

Wilted Love

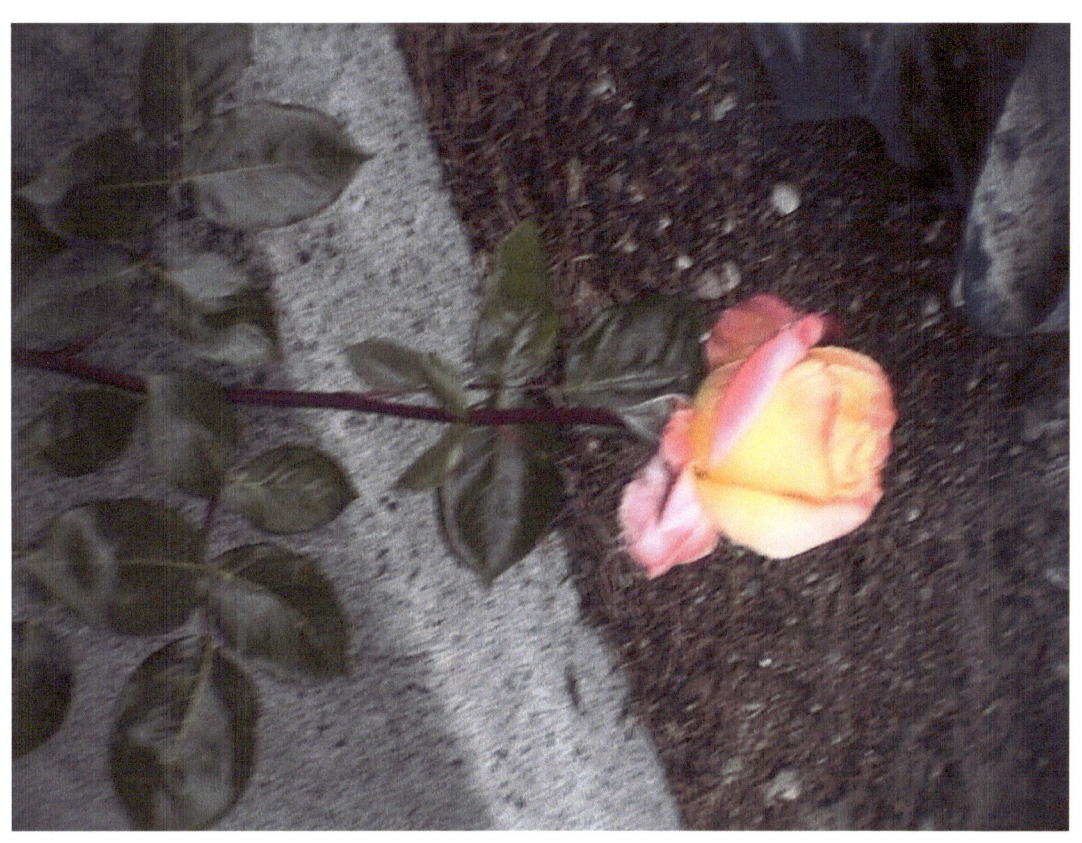

Mixture of Rough Edges

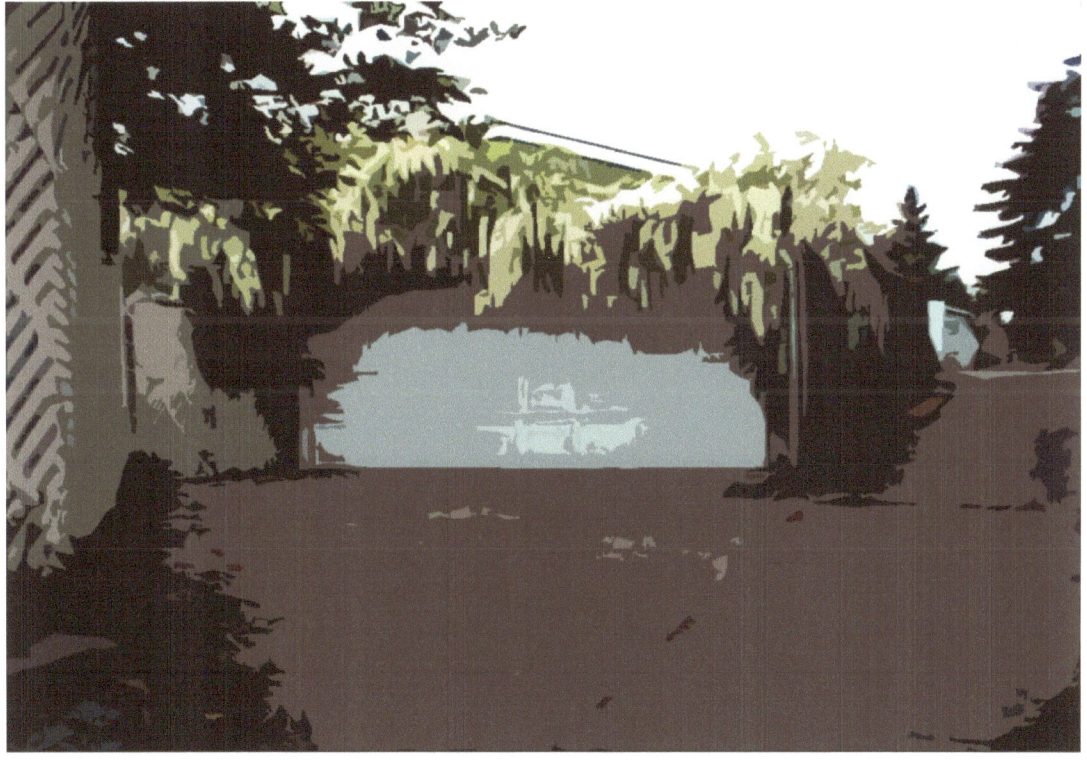

Painted Memories

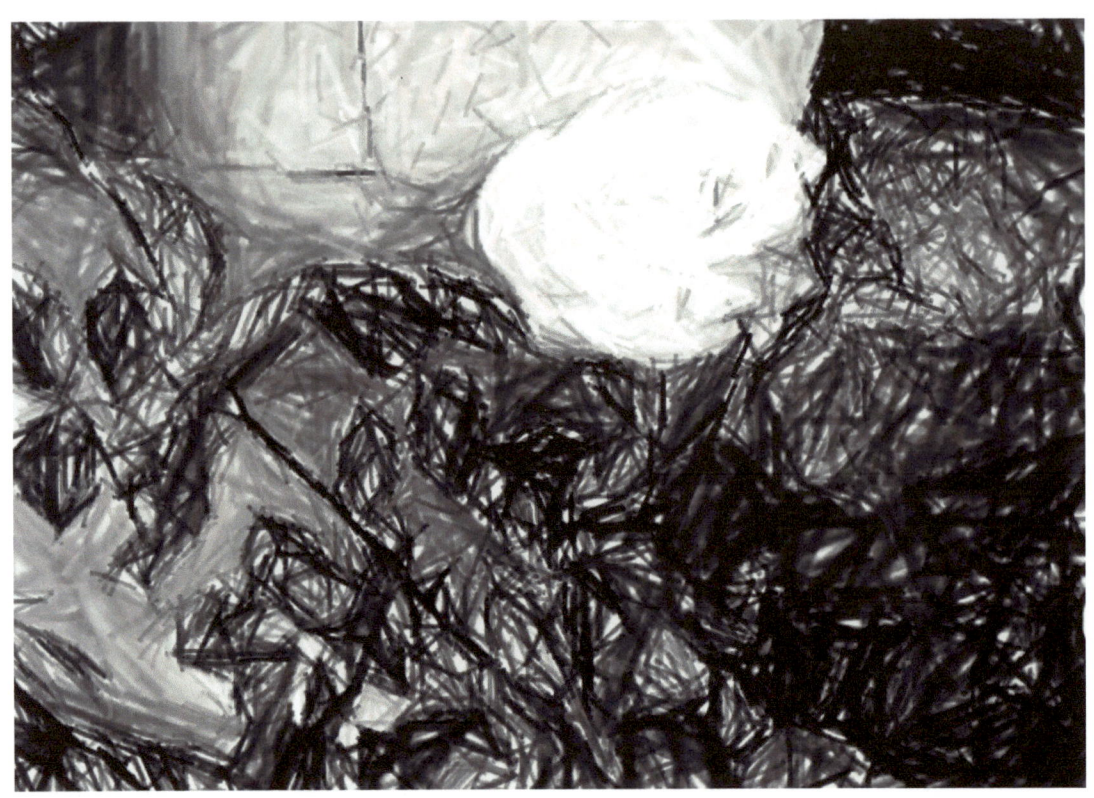

Scars and Trauma Standing

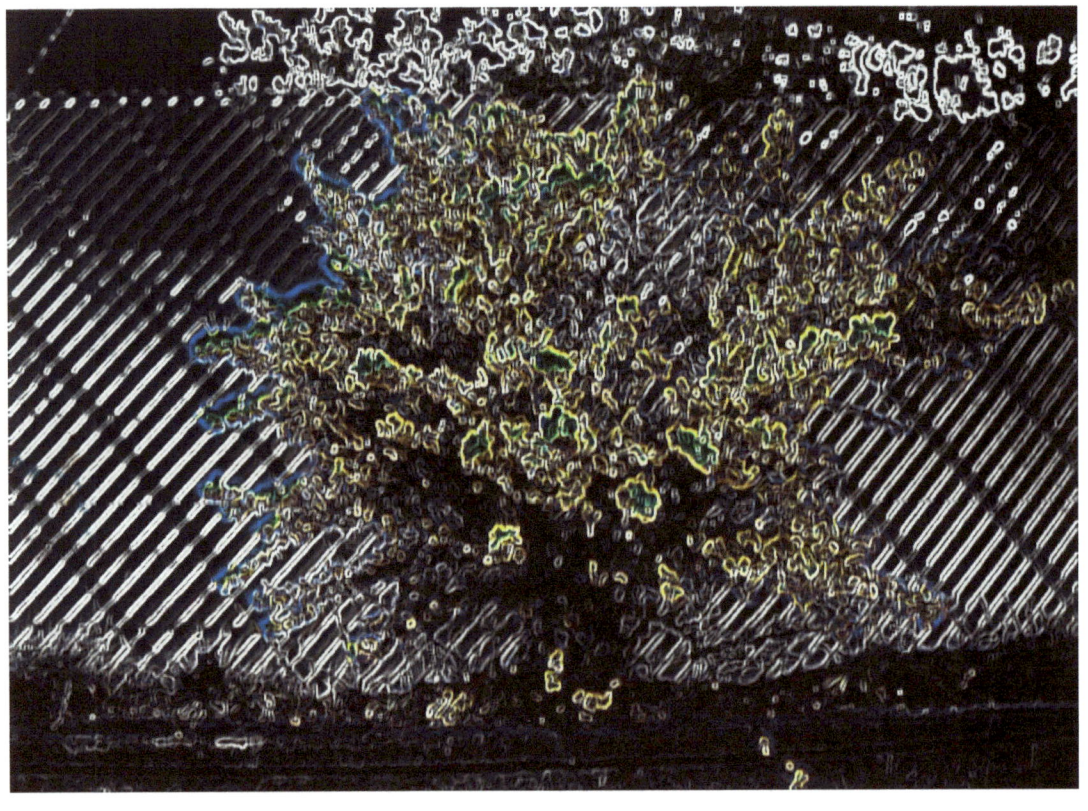

Pulling Energy

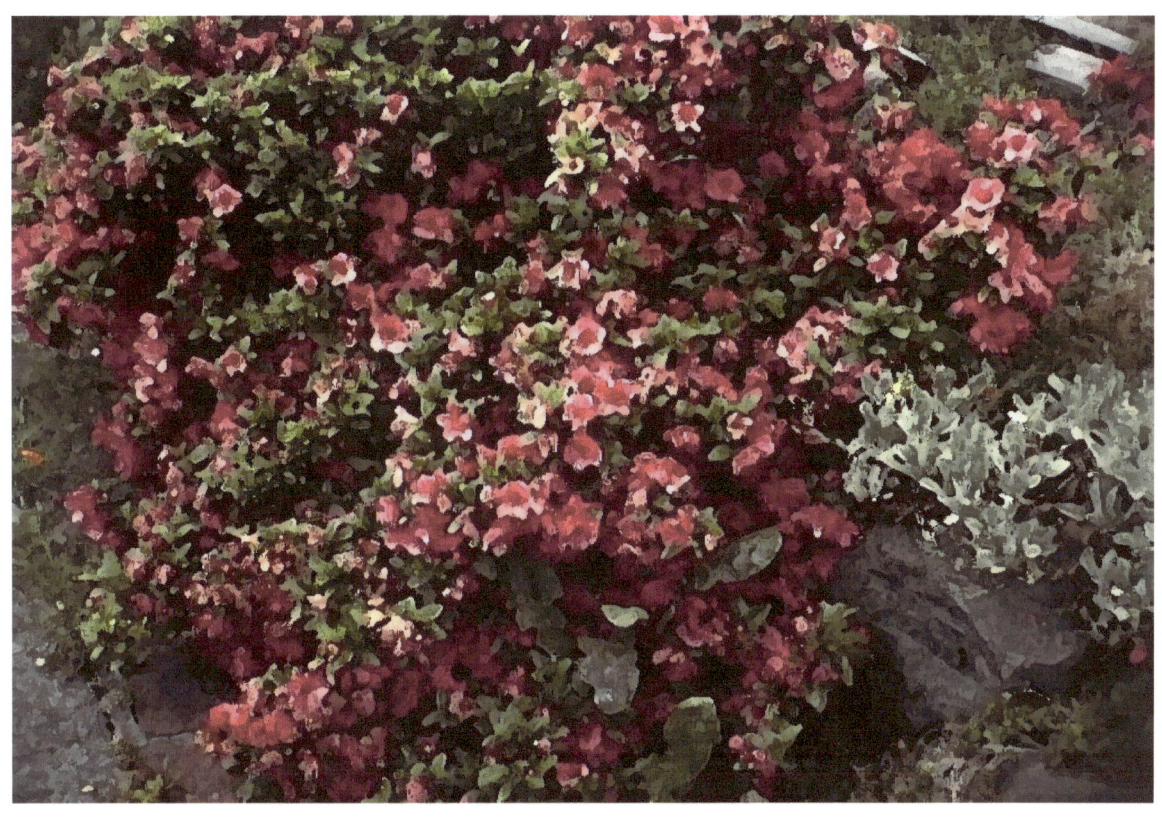

Paint Strokes of Living

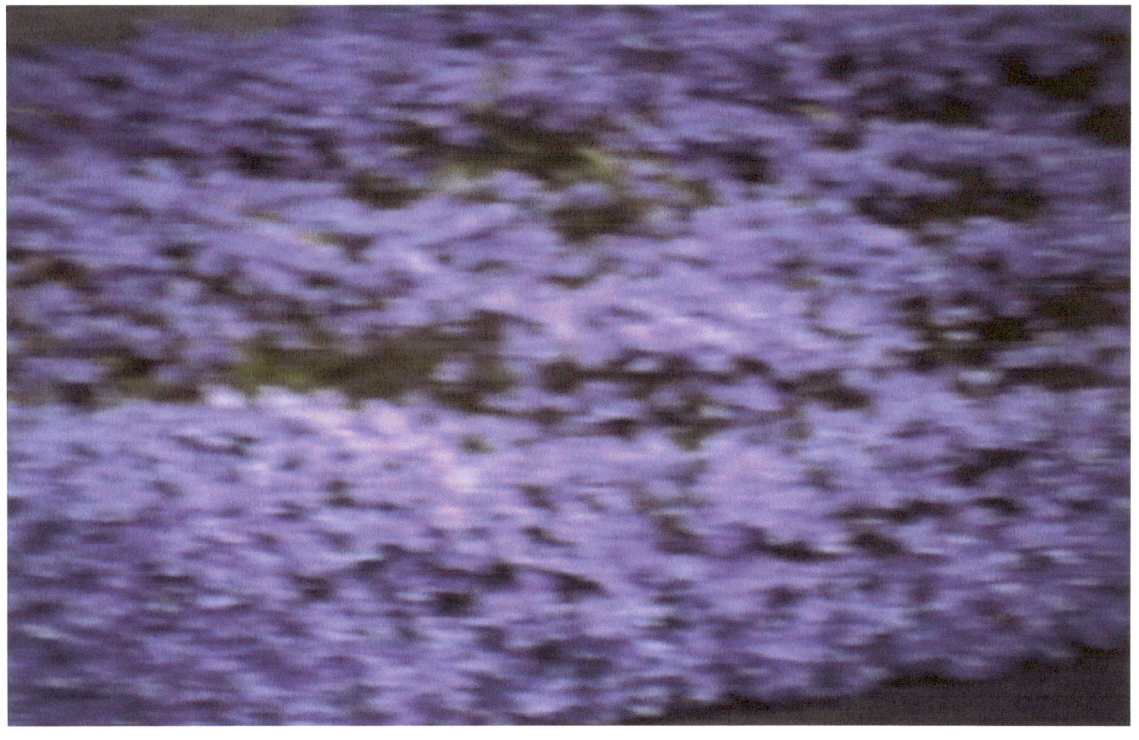

Emotional Contact

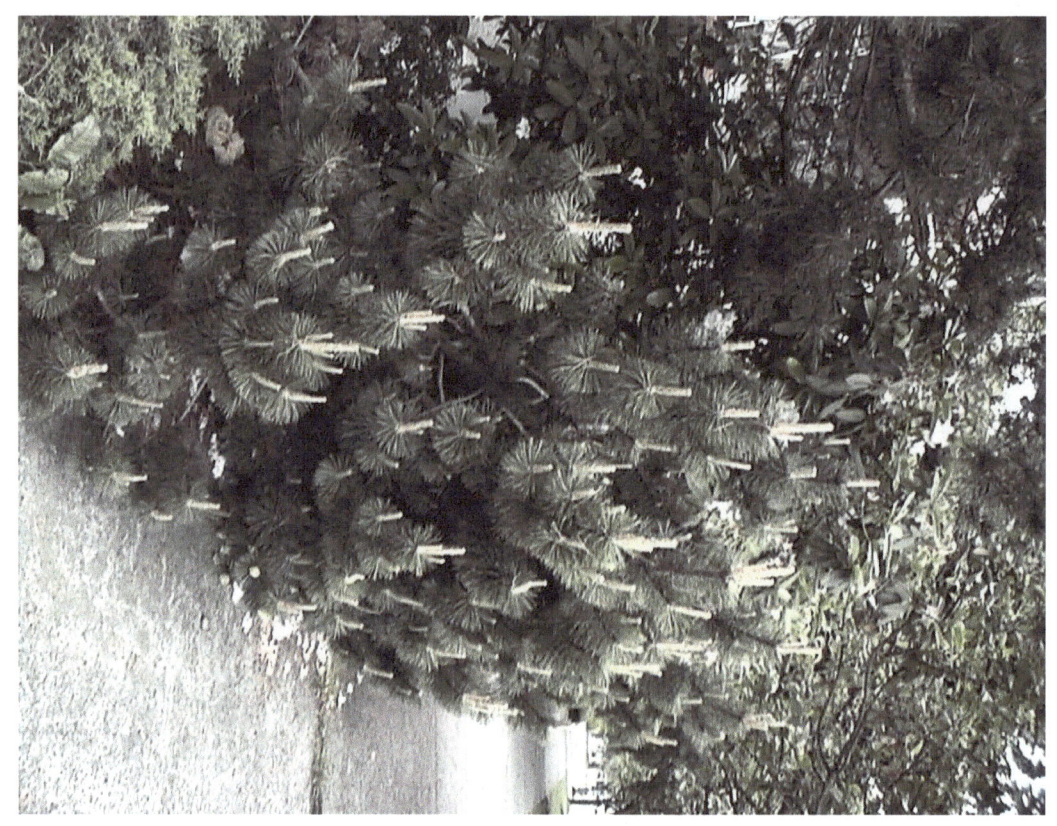
Twisted Politics Points

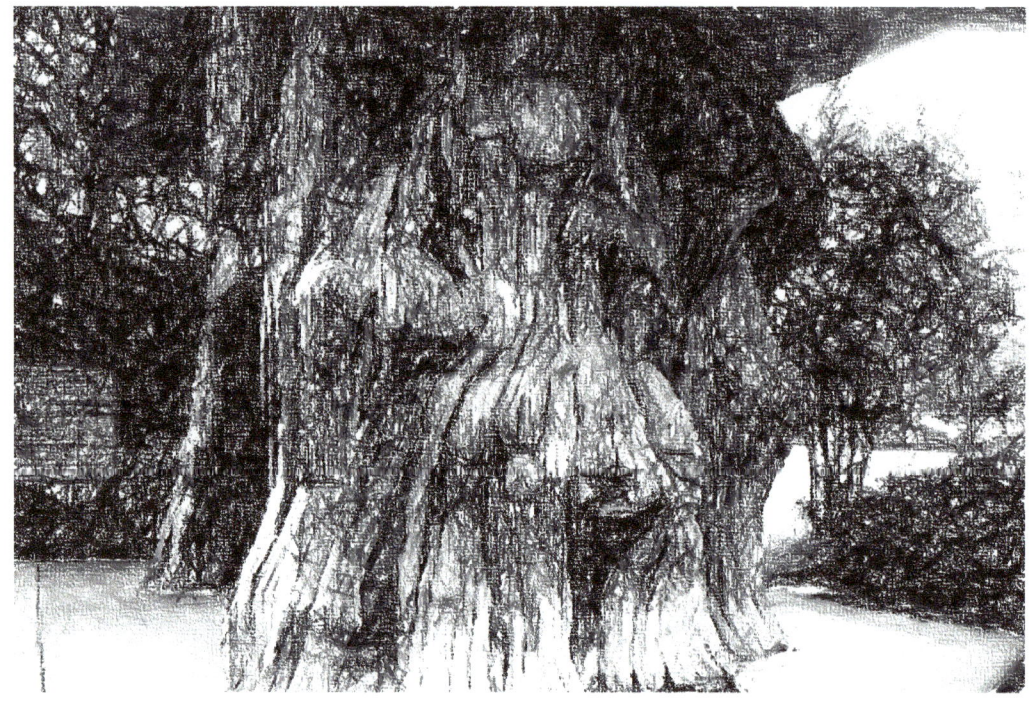
Artistic Expression

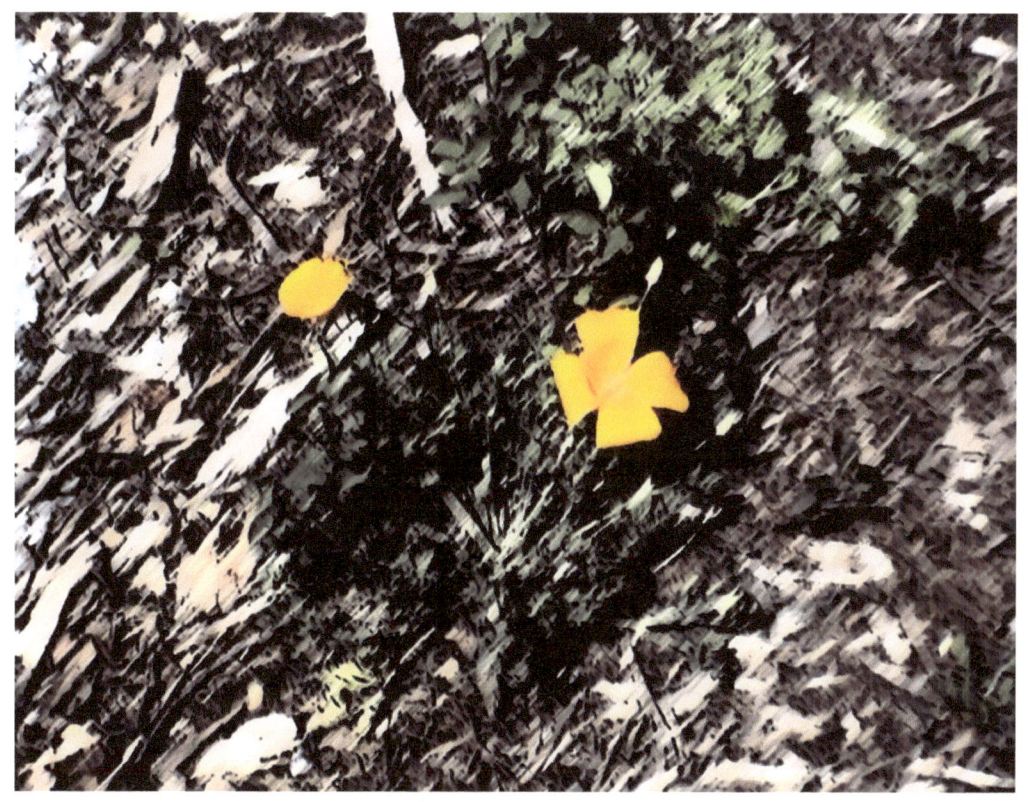

Twinkies Stand Out from the Normal

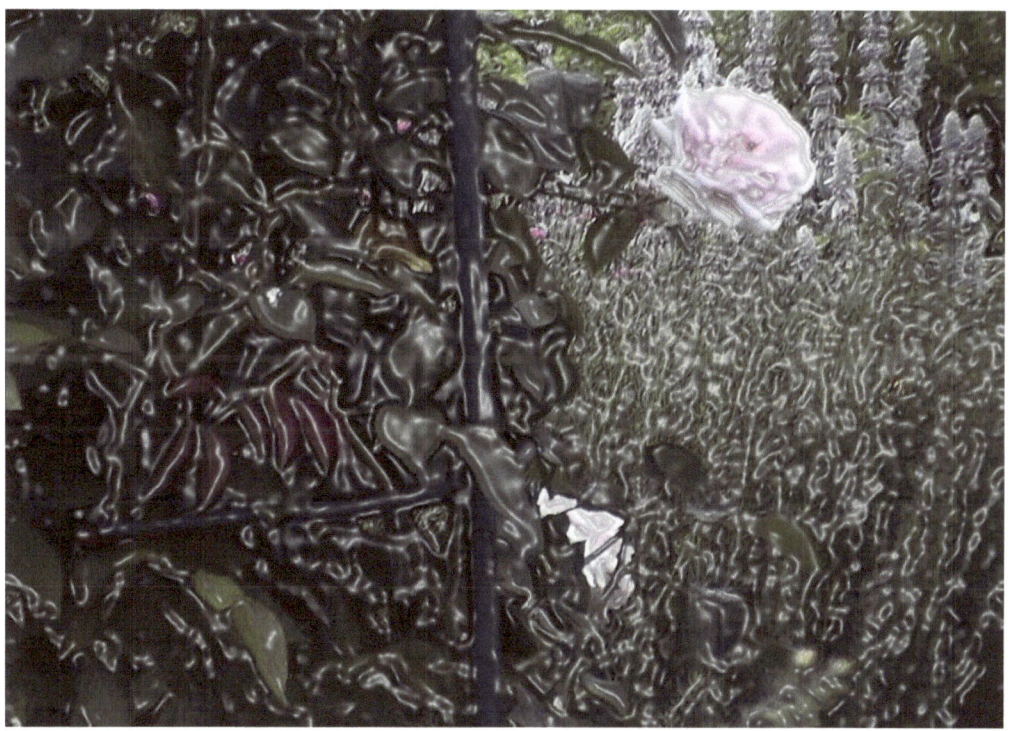

Melted Within

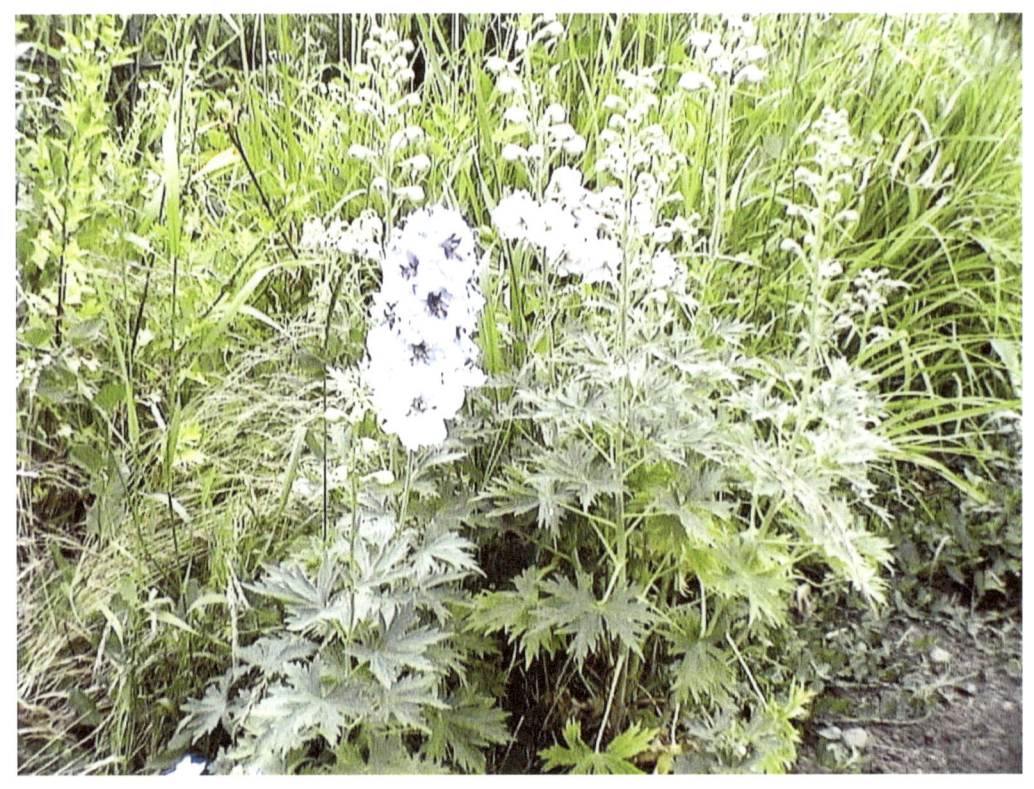

Vibrant Energy Emotions

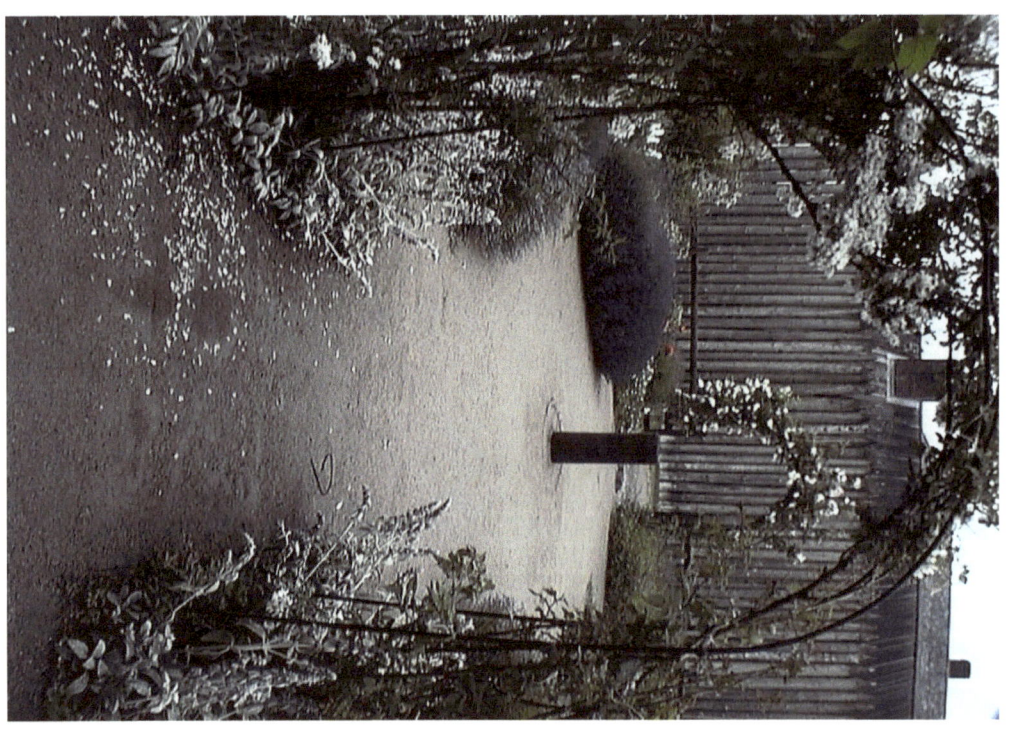

Understanding Curves

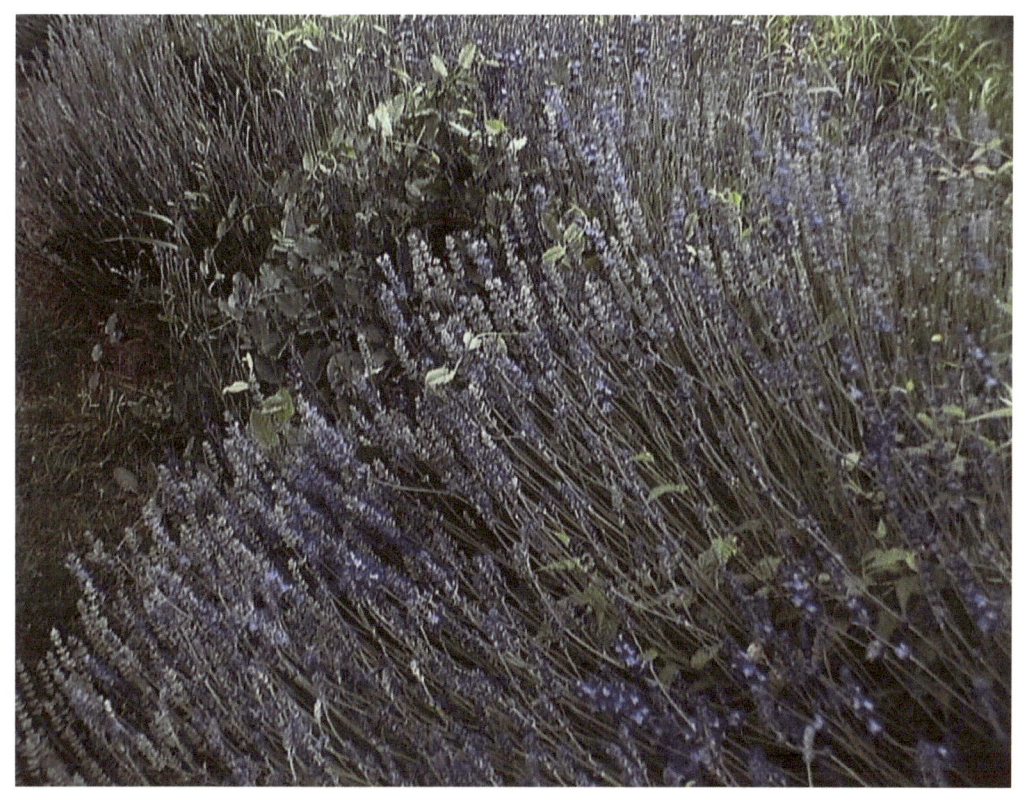

A Calling for Wisdom

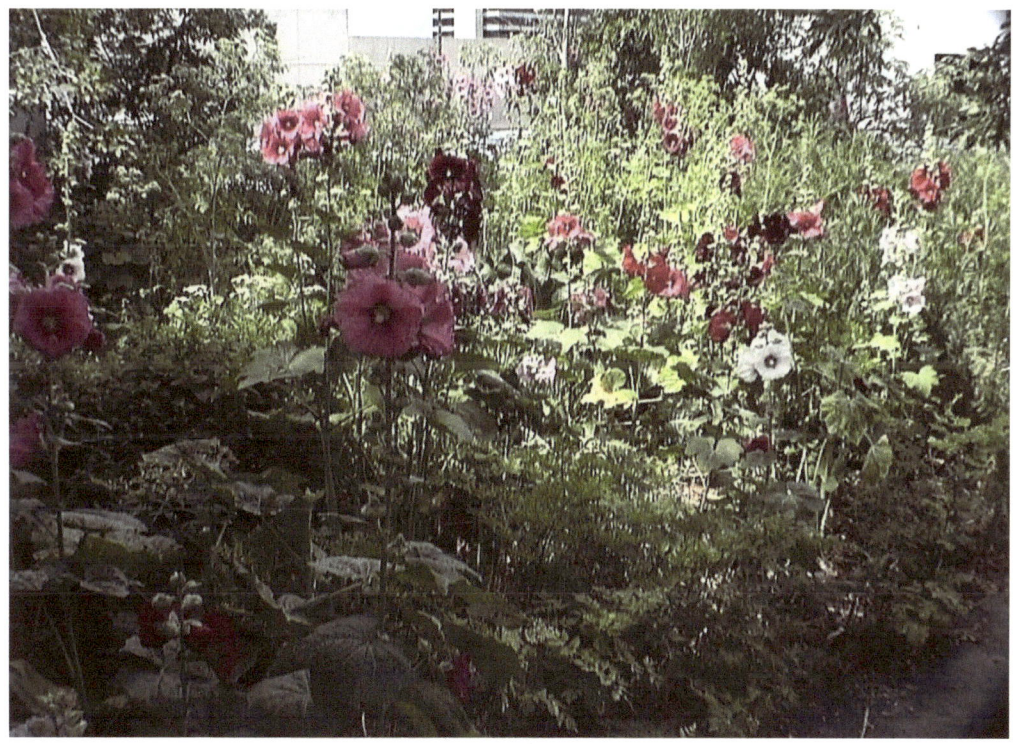

Clarity

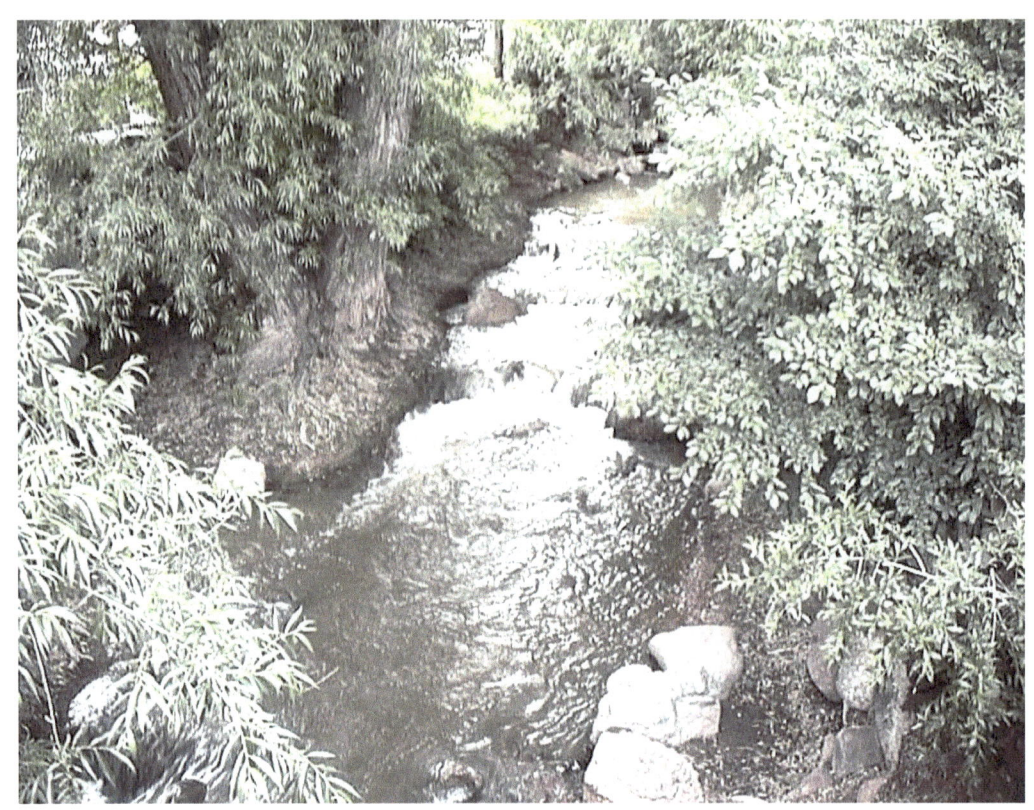

Streaming and Flowing Energy

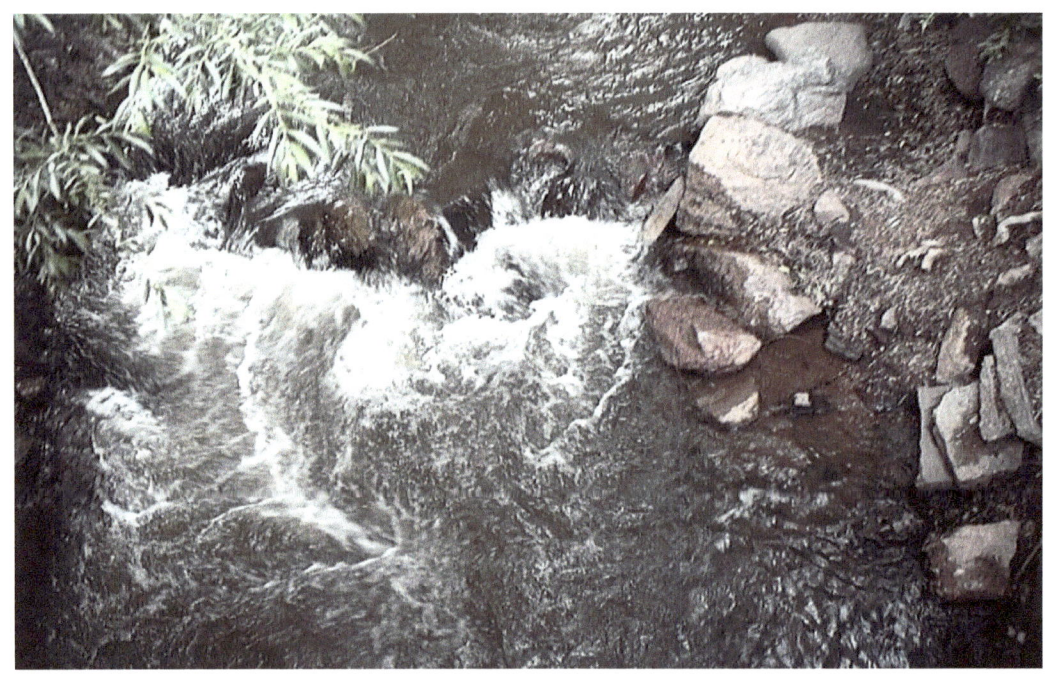

Focused Within

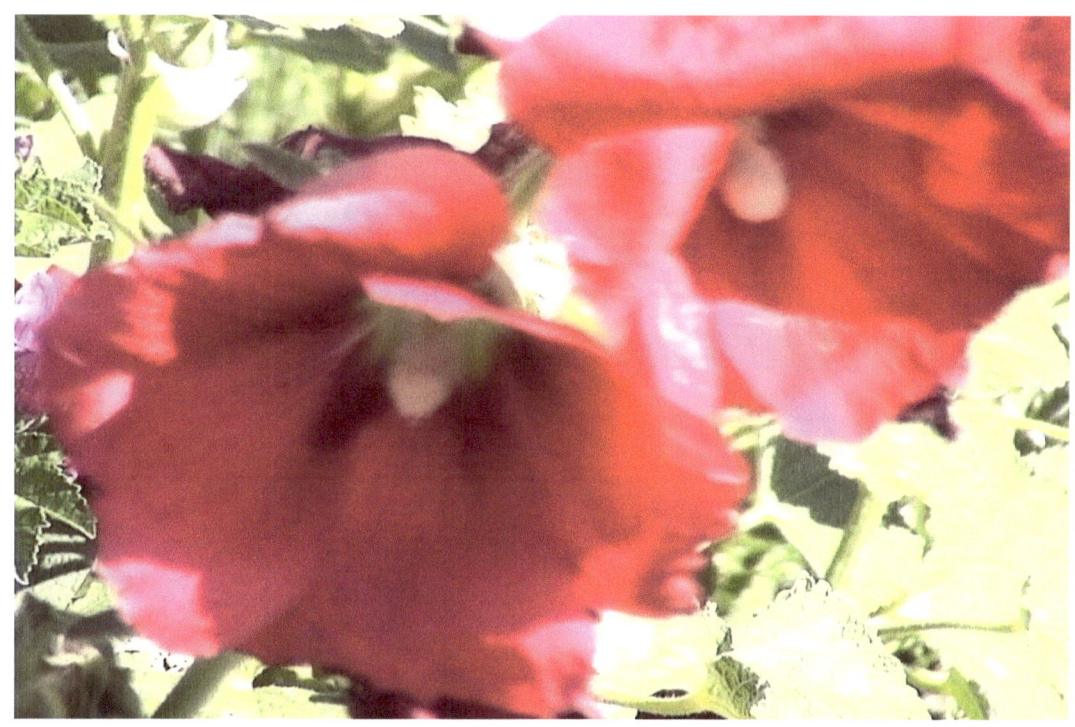

Bonded Together with Twisted Psychology

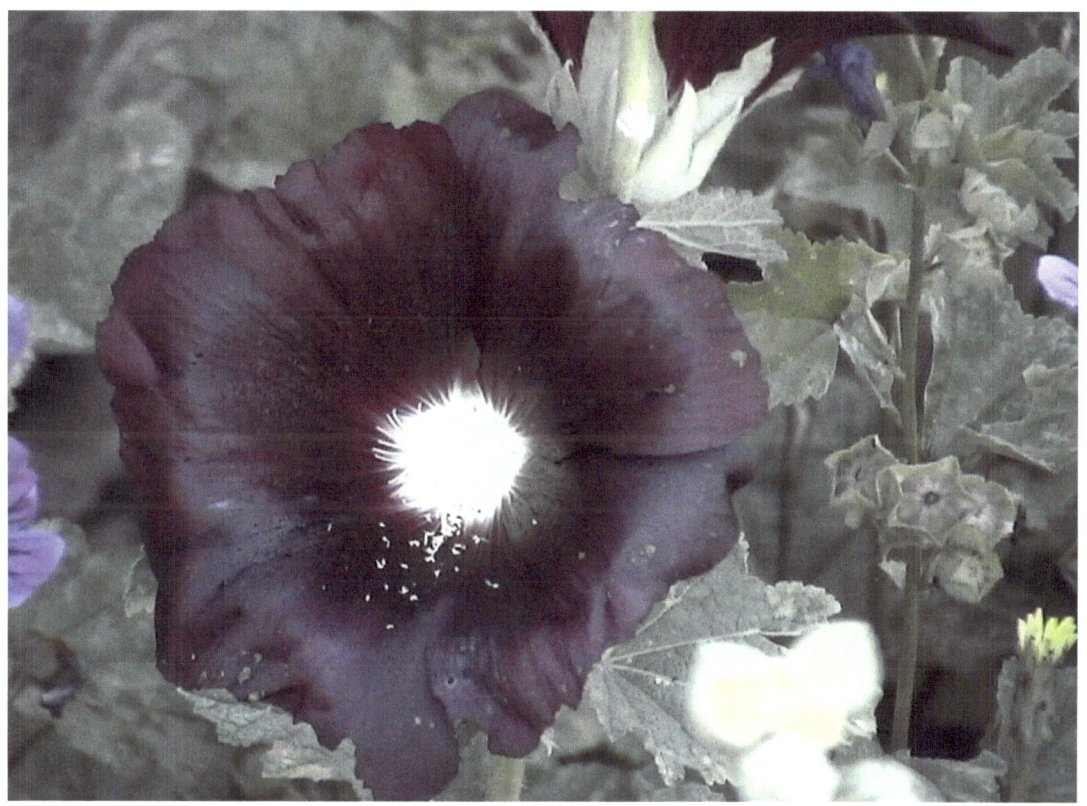

Opening the Soul

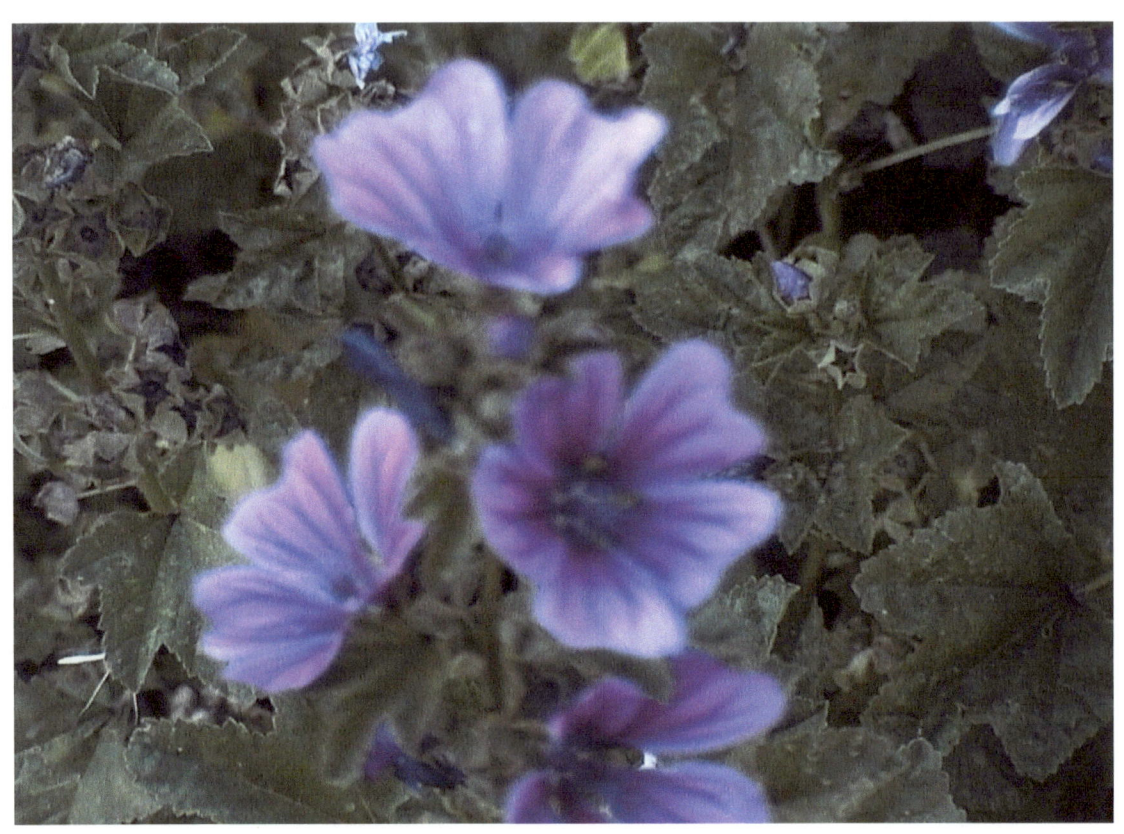

Standing in a Crowd with Confusion

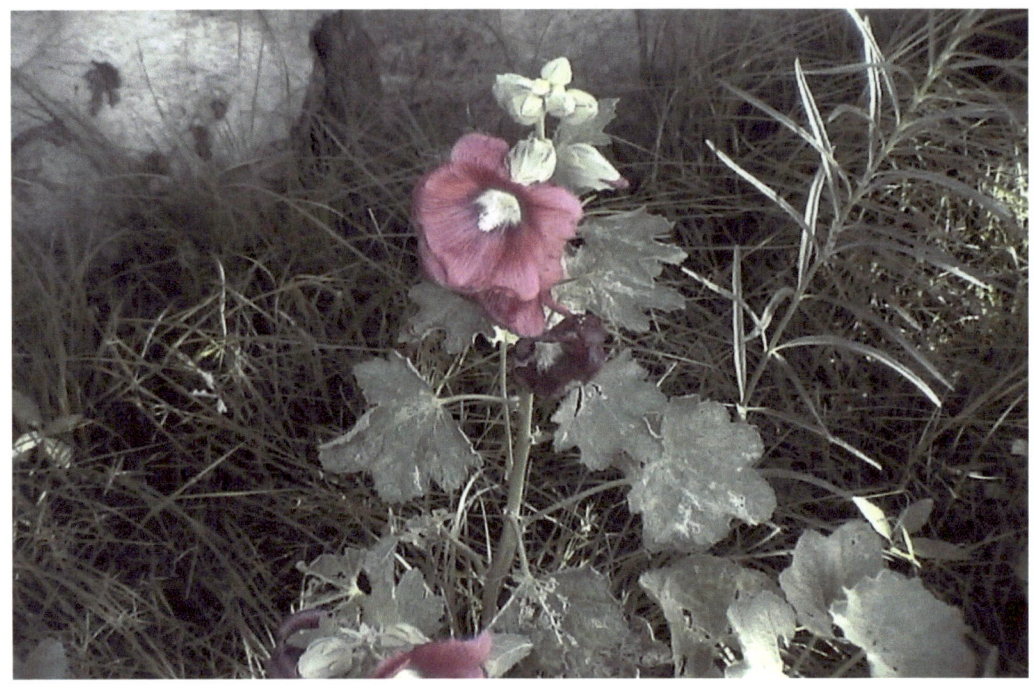

Blooming Beyond Your Own Values

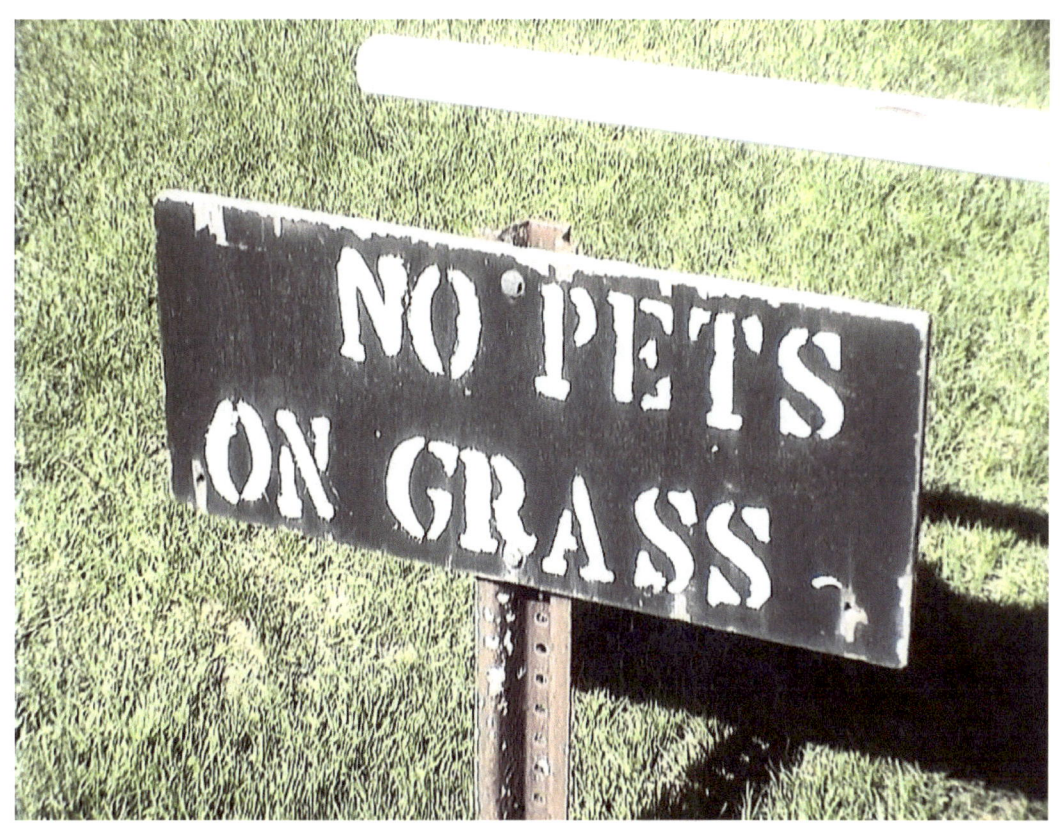

Lost Unity in Life

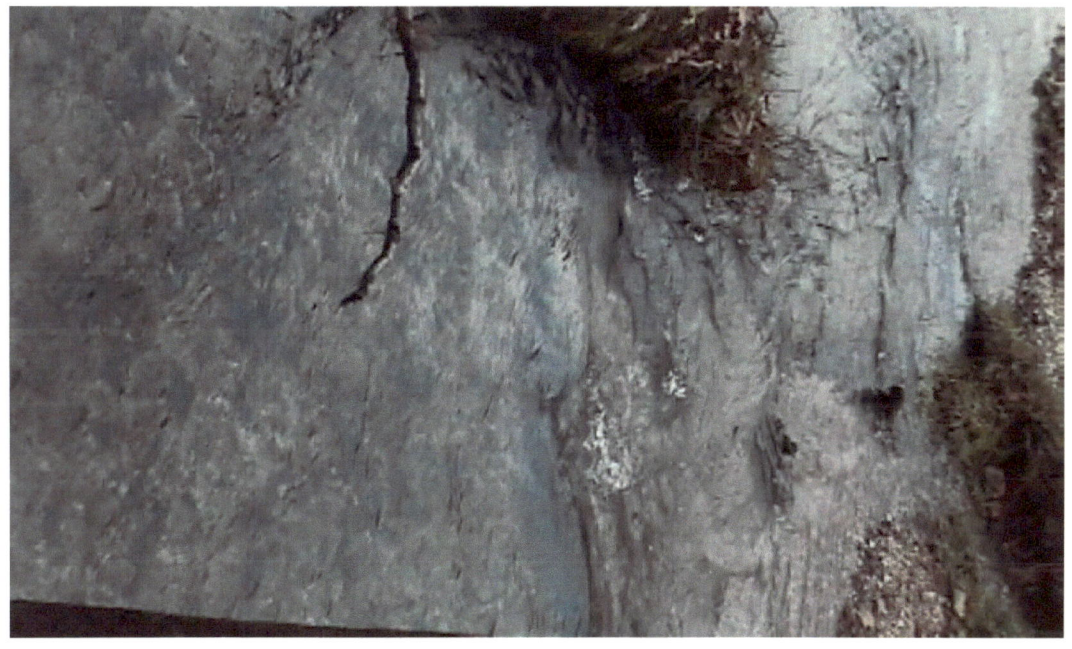

Solid Foundation Sideways

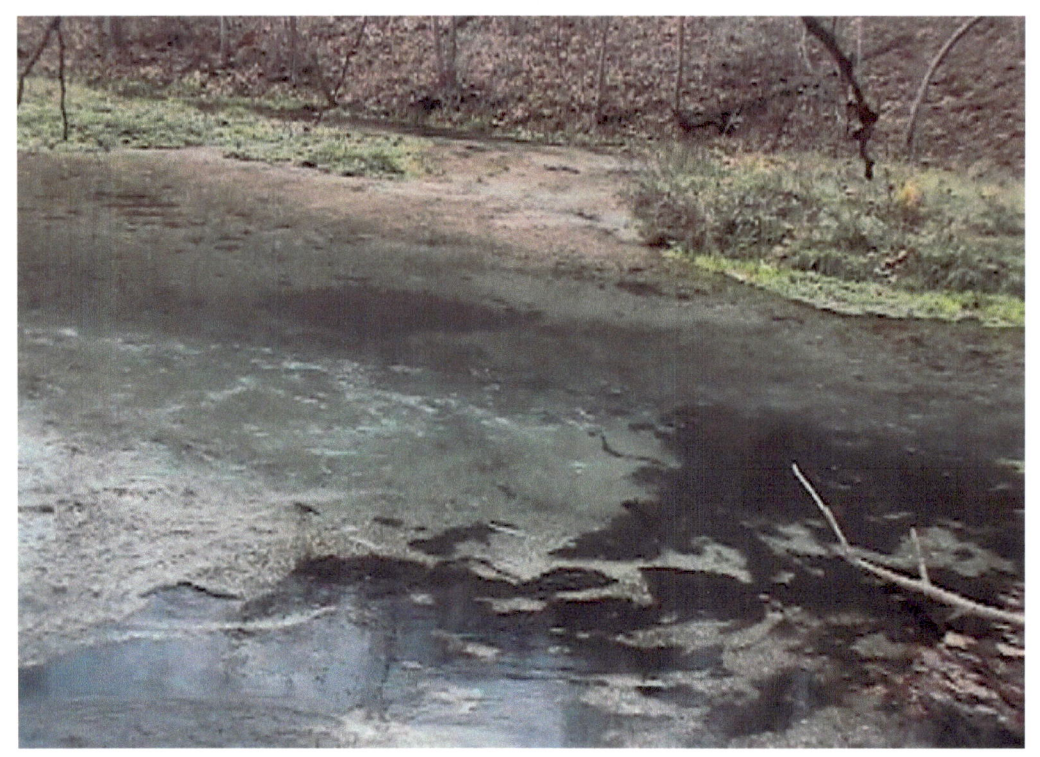

Breaking Down Reality

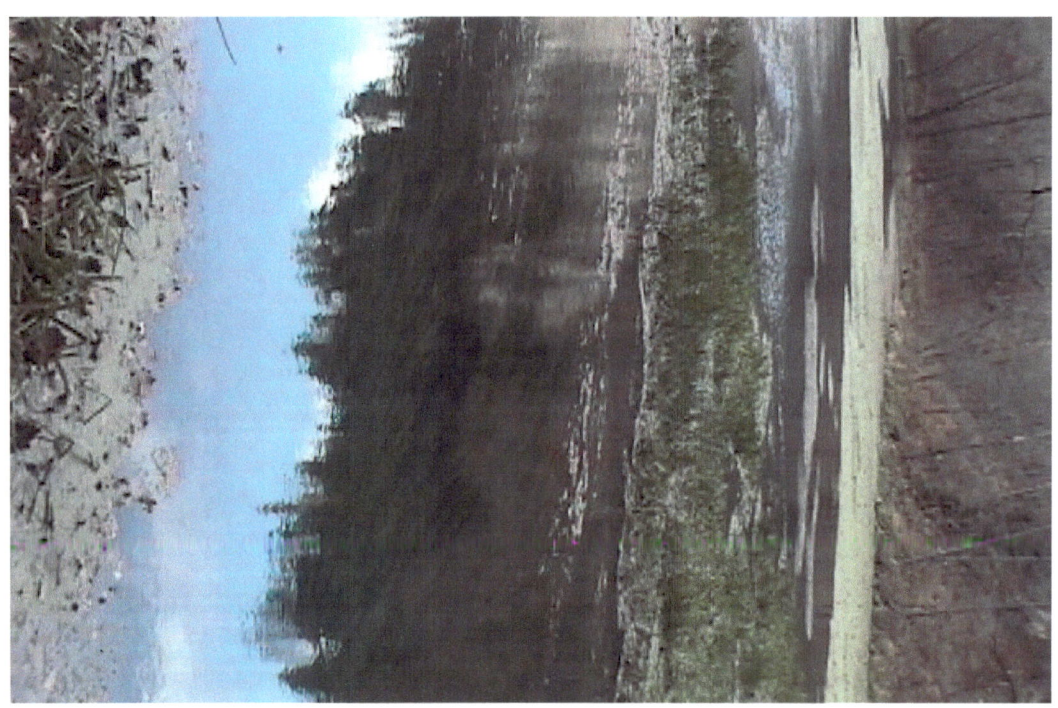

Flying Sideways

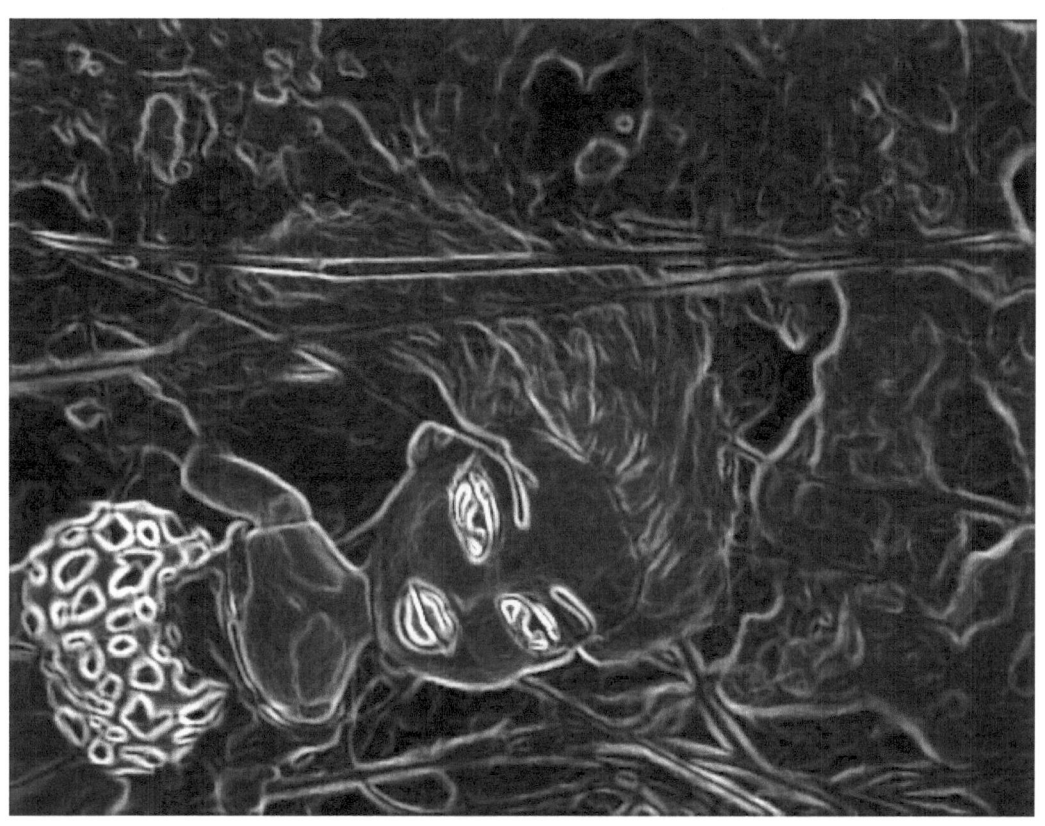

Can You Climb Out of Your Comfort Level?

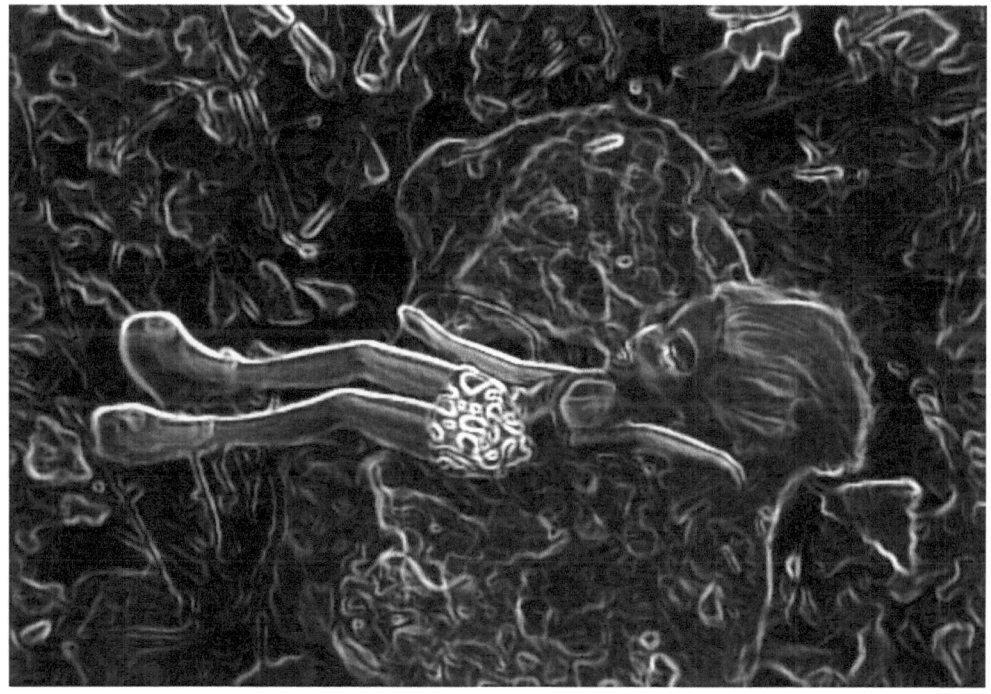

Secrets of Loving Outside the Normal

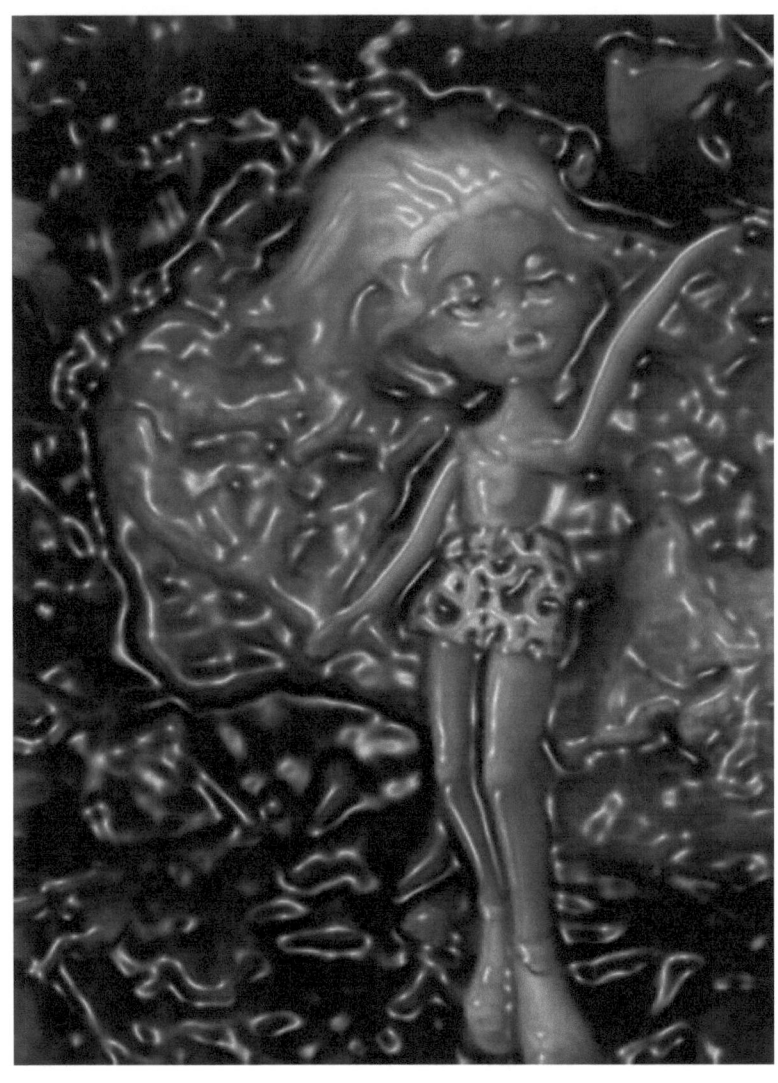

Beauty Melted in Addiction

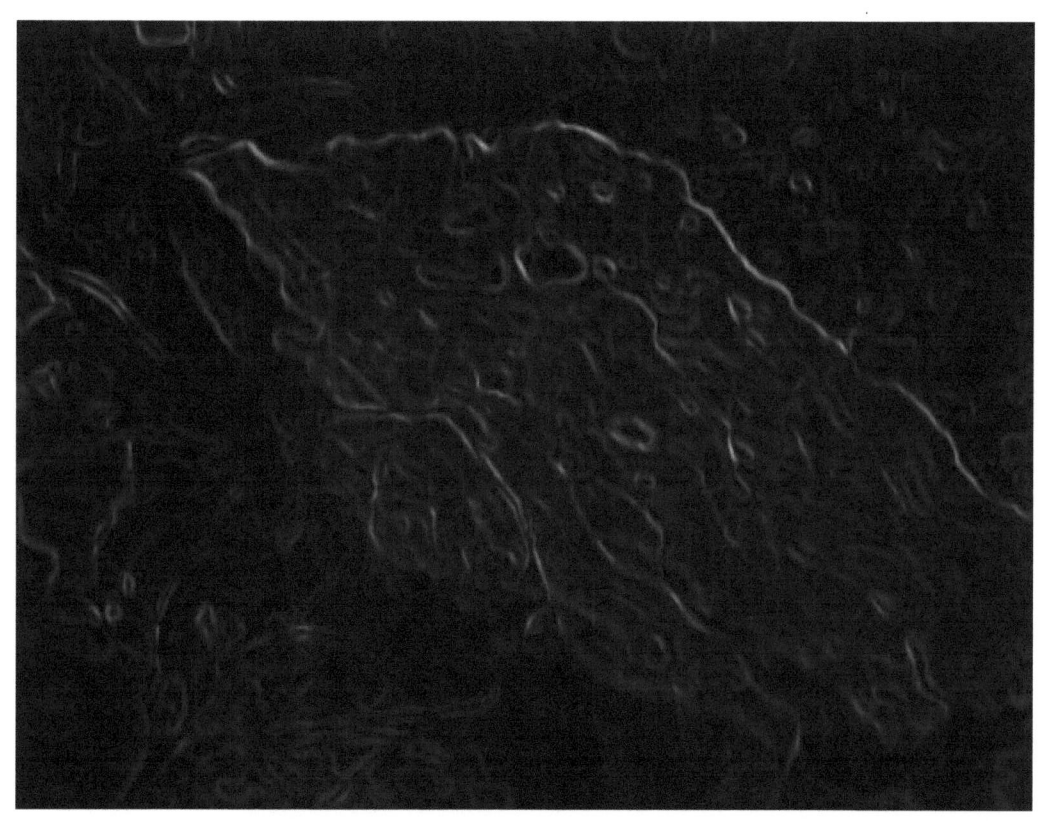

Edges of Lost Validation of Sexual Identity

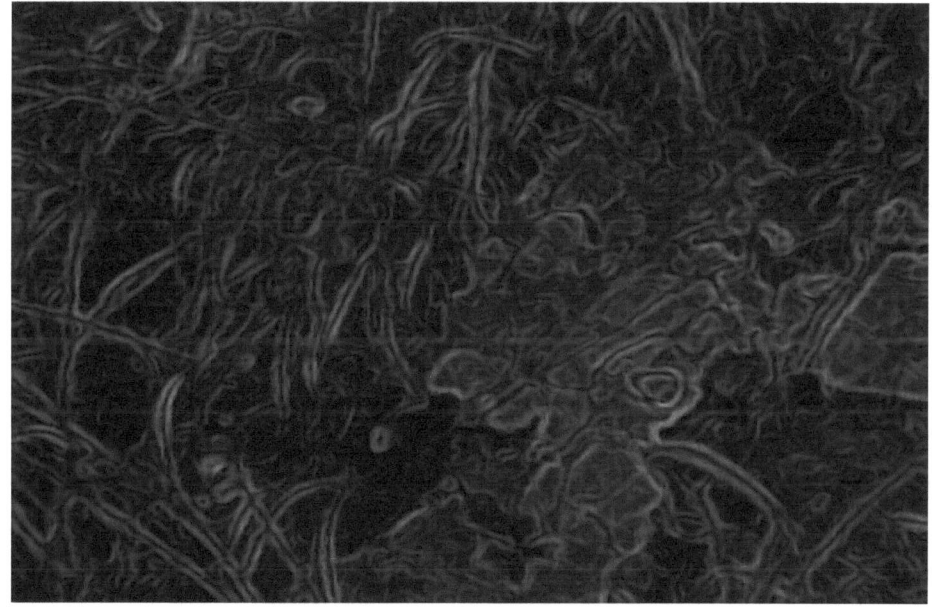

Weaving Through Life Without Nourishment

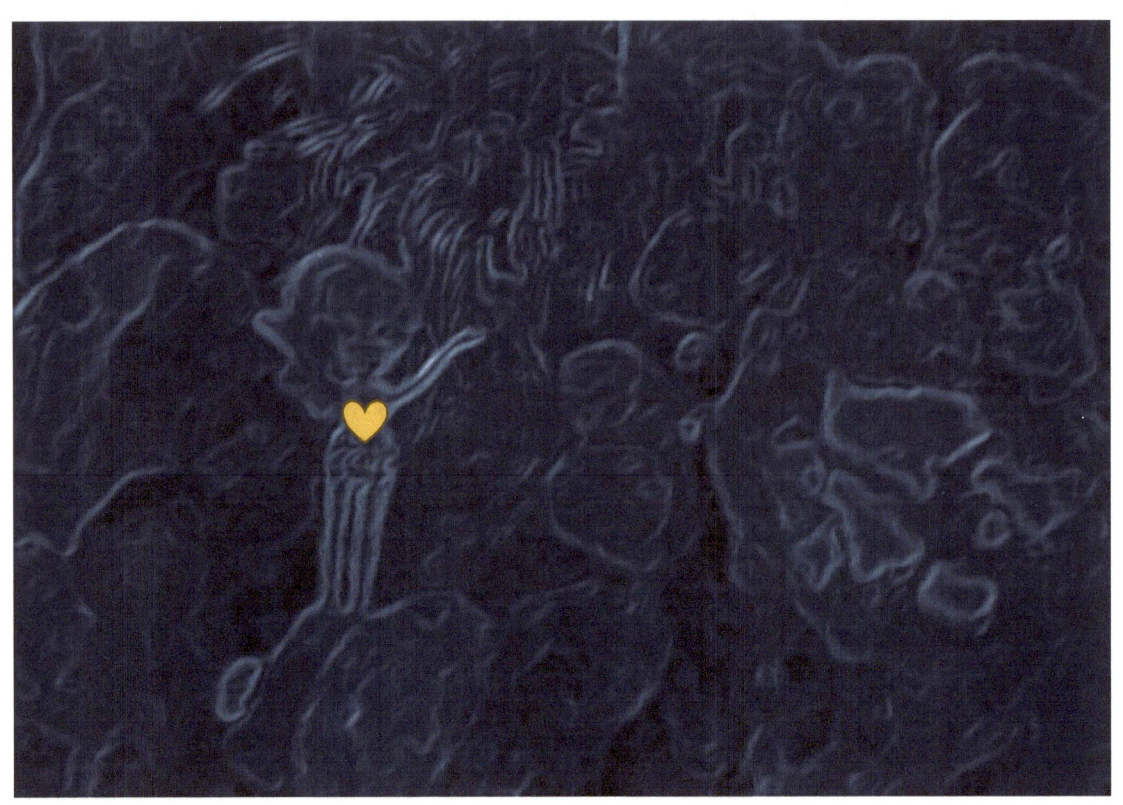

Curiosity Opening Up from the Dark

Seeing Colors with Confusion

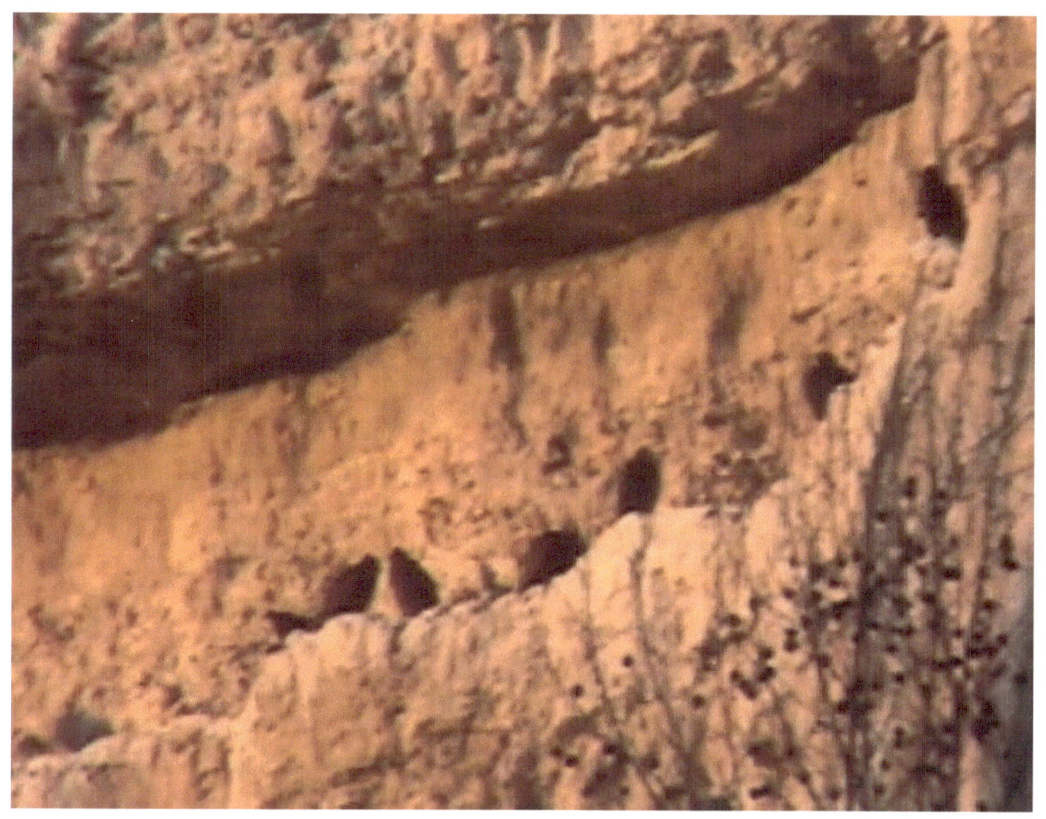

Connecting to Earth

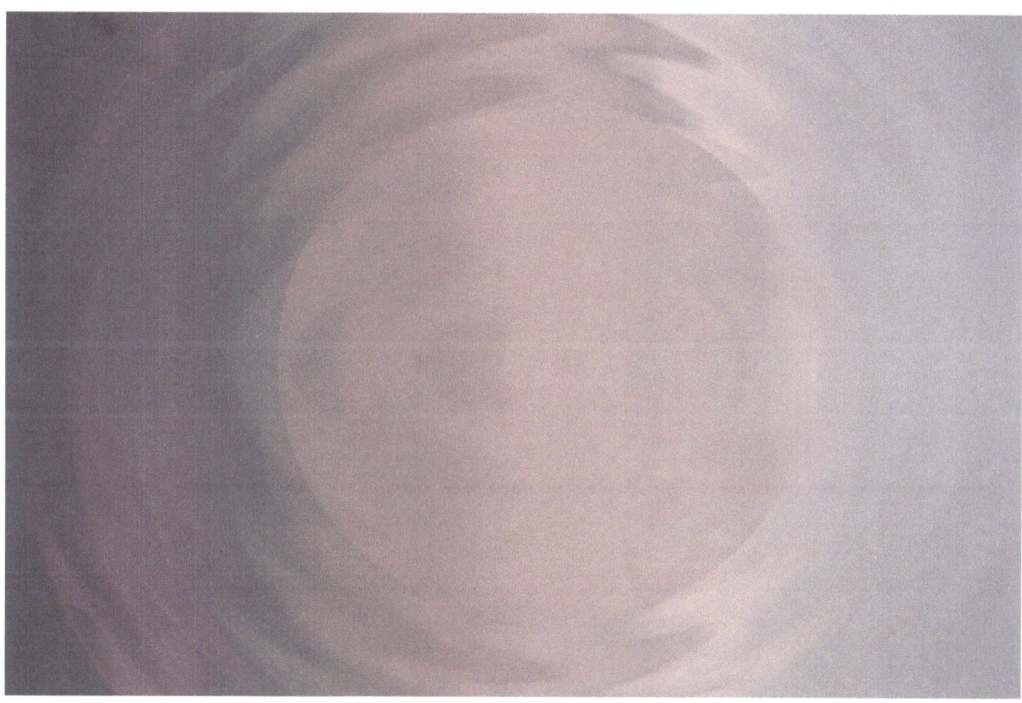

Finding Your Own Space in the Universe

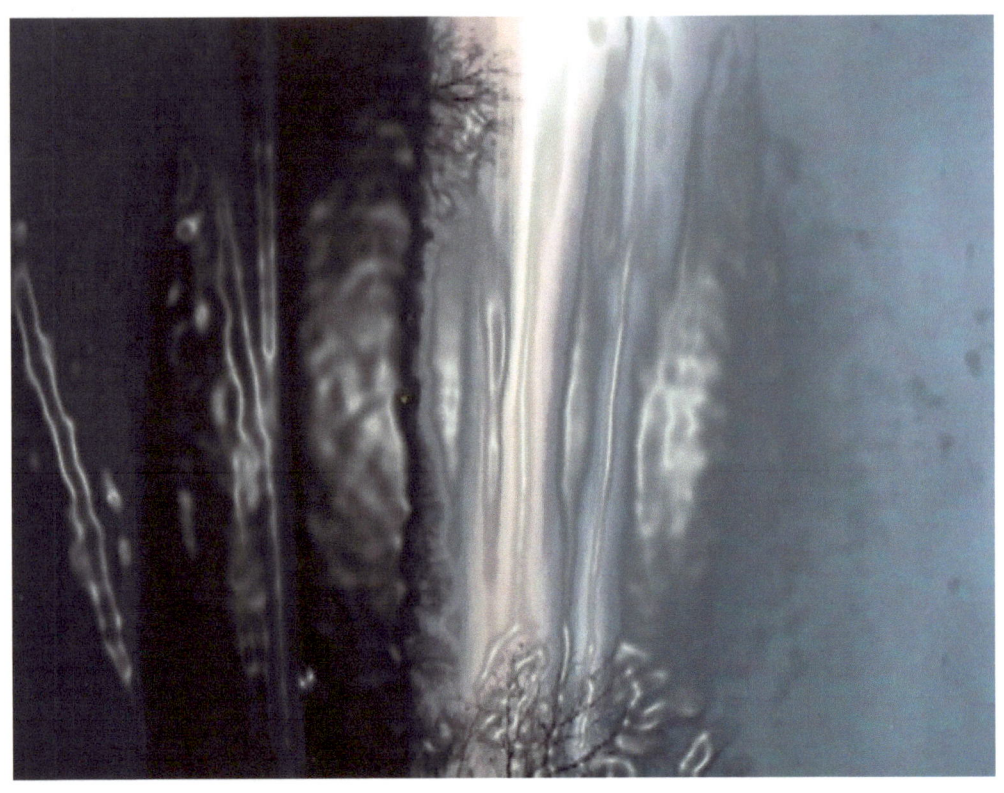

Center Grounding

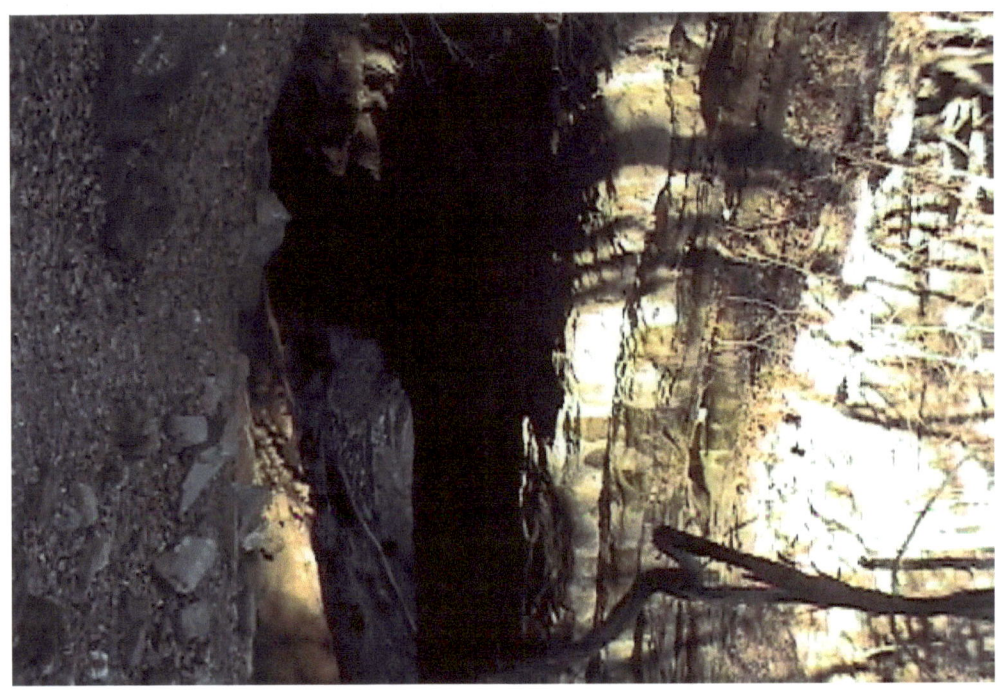

Can you see your inner child's Light awaken?

Seeds Planted in a Source

GROWS

Spiritually, Emotionally and Physically

Transitioning into another form of a simple realty is through transmutation, which means that you are growing and learning from another level of knowledge. Can you break open through your own stubbornness or comfort to find something more to life? It only takes one person to change their own direction, but it takes unity to change the volume of the world. Are you this person inside but are you afraid to climb up and out of the mentality of the unknown?

What If that: **WORLD**

Changes……. Changes…….Changes…..

You

Into Someone

Who Changes Something Ugly Into

Something

Beautiful

Can or Would you Challenge Yourself

To change you…………………………………..!!!!!!!!

www.ingramcontent.com/pod-product-compliance
Lightning Source LLC
Chambersburg PA
CBHW040057250526
45473CB00043B/1864